Legends of Rock & Roll

Eagles

An unauthorized fan tribute

By: James Hoag

 Published by www.number1project.com Monument Marketing Publishing LTD., 53 Hanover Dr., Orem, Utah 84058.

Paperback Edition

Manufactured in the United States of America

Also by James Hoag

Legends of Rock & Roll Volume 1 - The Fifties

Legends of Rock & Roll Volume 2 - The Sixties

Legends of Rock & Roll Volume 3 - The Seventies

Legends of Rock & Roll – Neil Diamond

(Available at Amazon.com)

TABLE OF CONTENTS

INTRODUCTION

"We set out to be a band for our time but sometimes when you do a good enough job, you become a band for all time." – Glenn Frey

I like to start these books out on a personal note. I can't remember when I was not an Eagles' fan: from their start in the early Seventies, when I was just a newly married man with a couple of young kids, until about five or six years ago when my wife and I saw them in person on their reunion tour; I don't think there is a song they did that I didn't like.

Eagles is an interesting group. Of the four who started the band, only two stayed with them all the way to the present (there is a short tour planned for this summer, 2013.)

There have been seven different performers who, at one time or another, could be called an Eagle. I will try to sort that all out and give you a ride through history as we discuss the beginnings, the peaks and valleys of the band, and the changes over the years.

Let's examine how the band came to be in the first place and then I will go back and discuss how each member got to the place where they would create a great band.

1-The Beginning of a Band

The band Eagles would have never happened if it weren't for the efforts of two people: Linda Ronstadt and her manager John Boyton. Glenn Frey and Don Henley were working as session musicians in the spring of 1971. Don was in a band called "Shiloh" which had originated in his native state of Texas. They were noticed by Kenny Rogers when he was in Texas, and he told them they should move to Los Angeles and try for a record deal. They did and produced one album which was a weak local hit but, otherwise, sank without much notice, so Shiloh broke up, and Don had to get work where he could.

Glenn Frey, who originally came from Michigan, was working with a country/ rock/ folk band called "Longbranch Pennywhistle," which was actually just two people: Glenn Frey and John David Souther (better known as J.D. Souther.) They did manage to record one album under a small California label and right after the album came out, the label went bankrupt and closed its doors. Without any support, the band broke up. Glenn and Souther remained friends and played together occasionally, but Longbranch Pennywhistle was pretty much a thing of the past.

Both Glenn Frey and Don Henley had played at a famous L.A. nightclub, The Troubadour. The Troubadour is located in West Hollywood, California and is famous for initiating the careers of many of the names we know from the Seventies. People like Elton John, Linda Ronstadt, James Taylor, and The Byrds all played at the Troubadour. Glenn and Don became acquainted while playing at the club.

The third member of the original four members of the band was Randy Meisner, who is originally from Nebraska. We'll discuss his history soon but in 1971, he was playing with the "Stone Canyon Band" which was Rick Nelson's backup band. Band members come and go, and Randy played with Nelson for a while and then quit for a while. He went home to Nebraska and then came back to Los Angeles. He, too, started playing at the Troubadour, and it was there that he met the other two guys: Glenn Frey and Don Henley.

The fourth member of the original group was Bernie Leadon, who is from a state I lived in for eighteen years: Minnesota. He, too, had been in several bands prior to 1971 but, just before becoming an Eagle, he was playing with the "Flying Burrito Brothers." They were a West Coast band that had quite a bit of success but was plagued by the same problems a lot of bands experience: constant changes in personnel. Bernie ended up playing for Linda Ronstadt, just like the other three.

So, the stage is set. We have the four original members of Eagles as they came together to play for Ronstadt. We have her to thank for the great music which was to follow. Let's see how each of the four got to this point.

2-DON HENLEY

Don was born Donald Hugh Henley on July 22, 1947 in Gilmer, Texas which is in the northeast corner of the state. Gilmer is the birth place of another great American singer, Johnny Mathis. Don is the son of Hughlene McWhorter and Con Junell (C. J.) Henley. He is an only child. As a young boy, the family moved about 45 miles northeast to the town of Linden, Texas where his father C. J. became the manager of the local NAPA auto parts store and where Don would spend the rest of his childhood.

Linden is about as close to the northeast corner of Texas as you can get. Due east about 25 miles is Louisiana, and Arkansas and Oklahoma are not too far to the north. When Don's family moved to Linden, it had a population of about 2,500 people. Linden, Texas was also the birthplace of two other great American musicians: Scott Joplin and T-Bone Walker. Don grew up listening to the music of the south. He could pick up WLAC out of Nashville that played all the R&B and rock and roll music of the Fifties and Sixties. He also listened to Wolfman Jack who broadcast just across the border in Mexico each night.

When I was in the Air Force in the early Sixties, I was stationed in Biloxi, Mississippi, and I remember these stations well. The radios we had in the rooms wouldn't pick them up, but the radio in the car would, so I spent many a night sitting in the driver's seat of my old 1955 Plymouth just listening to the radio listening to WLAC from Nashville because you could only pick it up after dark. Don Henley later wrote, "Music changed my life."

We might never have known Don except for the fact that he really wanted to play football. He tried out for the team at Linden-Kildare High School where he attended, but Don was not a big boy. In fact, he was kind of thin and scrawny. The coach told him football was just not in the cards. Discouraged, he wanted to join something, so he joined the school band.

He started out on the trombone but soon the band conductor noticed that Don was always drumming on his books and every other surface he could find, so he moved Don from trombone to drums, and that's where Don has been ever since. He played school drums, but they weren't that good so one day his mother told him to get in the car, and they drove to a nearby town where she bought him a brand new set of Slingerland Red Sparkle drums which Don still owns today.

Put drum sticks in a boy's hands and the first thing he wants to do is start a band, so Don got together with a couple of buddies from school, and they formed "The Four Speeds" (I assume named after the four speeds on a gear shift.) At first, they couldn't decide who should be the lead singer. No one wanted to do it, so they literally drew straws, and Don drew the short straw and became the vocalist.

After graduating from high school, Don attended Stephen F Austin University in Nacogdoches, Texas and then a year later transferred to North Texas State University in Denton, Texas. He only took one music course while in college, and he flunked it, but he says he didn't really care because he was an English major. The band played on, however, as they went from place to place. The personnel changed and even the name of the band changed (to "Felicity"), but Don kept going.

One day, believe it or not, they were shopping at a boutique in Dallas when Kenny Rogers walked in. Kenny Rogers was still with First Edition at this time. They got to talking, and Don asked Rogers to come hear them at a local bar where they were playing. At first Rogers said, "Oh, I don't do that," but Don was persuasive, and Rogers agreed to come see them. Rogers apparently liked what he heard because he told them to come to L.A., and he would support them in making their first record. They could even stay at his house, so the guys packed up and moved to L.A.

With the help of Kenny Rogers, they changed their name once again this time to "Shiloh" and cut their first record called, "Jennifer." They recorded one album as Shiloh, a self-titled album for Amos Records which was a small independent label in Los Angeles. Nothing much happened with the album. Amos probably couldn't afford to promote it and the band kind of drifted apart.

Don spent a lot of his time at The Troubadour where he met Glenn Frey along with Linda Ronstadt, Neil Young, and Jackson Browne. Ronstadt had asked Glenn to be part of her back up band and he, in turn, asked Don to join them. Glenn told Don that he could earn $200 a week on the road touring with Ronstadt, so Don joined Ronstadt's band.

3-Glenn Frey

Glenn Lewis Frey was born on November 6, 1948 in Detroit, Michigan to Nellie and Edward Frey. His father worked as a factory worker in the auto industry and his mother baked pies for General Motors. He grew up in Royal Oak, Michigan which is a nice suburb outside of the city of Detroit. His mother, Nellie, was a fan of big band music and he is named after Glenn Miller, down to the two Ns.

Glenn had two younger brothers: Alan and Matt. There is some controversy as to whether Matt Frey is really his brother but after much searching on the internet, I have come to the conclusion that he is his brother (and should not be confused with the Matt Frey who is in the current hot teen band "Big Time Rush".).

Glenn literally grew up on the streets of Detroit. The streets were safer then than they are today but being small in stature, he was still beat up on a regular basis. He started taking piano lessons when he was five and that contributed to the bullying. As he got older, he became interested in sports and that helped him to avoid the bullies. He stopped playing the piano when he was twelve. When he was thirteen, his brother, Alan, accidently hit him in the nose with a baseball bat, breaking it.

Glenn wanted to learn the guitar but hadn't got around to it until he happened to see The Beatles perform when they came to the United States in 1964. He did not see them on television; he saw them in person, something I have always been sorry I didn't do when I had the chance. He watched in amazement as the girls screamed and fainted over the sight of the group. He knew right then that this was what he wanted to do, so he bought an acoustic guitar and started a band just like a lot of high school kids do. After being in several bands, mostly amateur musicians who faded away, he got together with some guys who called themselves "Mushroom." This band did a little better and Glenn was able to work at some of the nightclubs in the Detroit area.

It was while playing with Mushroom that he met Bob Seger. Seger was just getting started in Detroit, and his band was called "The Bob Seger System." Mushroom broke up, and Glenn played with other bands like the Four of Us, the Subterraneans, and the Heavy Metal Kids.

Glenn tried to go to college, but his heart just wasn't in it. He would rather spend his time playing, chasing girls, and smoking marijuana. When he was nineteen, he had the opportunity to play with Bob Seger again on the song "Ramblin' Gamblin' Man." This was Seger's first hit record and actually made the Top 40, peaking at number seventeen. Glenn was a part of The Bob Seger System when this song was recorded. He plays and sings background for Seger. You can hear the song on YouTube and if you listen for the background singers, one of them is Glenn Frey.

Glenn finally decided that if he was going to make it big in the music business, he needed to go to California. That was where it was happening. He later stated, "I read about free love and dope in California so at age 20, I drove to Los Angeles." In L.A., he got together with another hopeful named John David Souther (or as he became known in the music world, J.D. Souther.) Souther was also from Detroit and was dating the sister of Glenn's girlfriend at the time. Souther was a little ahead of Glenn in the business and so showed him the ropes. They tried composing together and eventually formed a two-man group that they called "Longbranch Pennywhistle."

If you've heard of Longbranch Pennywhistle then you are a true fan. They did record one album together which had a country-rock feel to it. Do a search for Longbranch Pennywhistle on YouTube and listen to some of their music. I think it's pretty good. Their style of music, of which we will hear much more when the Eagles come together, was just a little early and while they got some attention, the first album only generated one local hit, "Run Boy Run" which did not make any charts nationally.

The boys kept trying, however, playing at all the local clubs where country/folk/rock was encouraged and this included the Troubadour. They got to know Jackson Browne from the Troubadour. Browne had been a member of the Nitty Gritty Dirt Band and was now on his own. He wrote his own music and seemed to be going places, so Glenn and J.D. asked him to move in with them. Glenn and J.D. occupied the upstairs of their house and Browne lived in the basement.

Glenn says he would sit upstairs and listen to Browne compose music and by listening to him, Glenn learned how to compose himself. Glen relates the story this way: Jackson Brown would sit at the piano and play the same verse over and over, twenty or more times until he got it just the way he wanted it. Then, he would write it down and go on to the next verse and play that over and over. Glenn says by listening to Browne, he learned how to compose music.

Jackson Browne was friends with Linda Ronstadt who performed at the Troubadour and so the guys got the opportunity to meet Ronstadt and play with her. From there, Glenn met Don, and we are now to the same place in history we were before.

Footnote: J.D. Souther, went on to be a part of The Souther, Hillman, Furay Band who had a Top 40 hit with, "Fallin' in Love" (#27) in 1974. He then had a solo hit which most people remember who listened to music in the Seventies, "You're Only Lonely" which peaked at number seven in 1979, so J.D. had his own career.

4-RANDY MEISNER

Randy Herman Meisner was born March 8, 1946 in Scottsbluff, Nebraska, the son of Emilie and Herman Meisner. His parents were sharecroppers and that basically means poor. Working the land in Nebraska can take a toll on people. To my knowledge, he only had one sibling, a sister named Carol.

Like so many before him, Randy got interested in music by watching television. He saw Elvis Presley on *The Ed Sullivan Show* and decided that was what he wanted to do, so he saved his money, bought a guitar, and began to teach himself to play.

He and some friends had founded a band called, The Dynamics, and they got some local attention. The Dynamics played their first concert in October of 1961, and they played together through much of 1962. They changed their name to the Drivin' Dynamics and actually released an EP (Extended Play) of their work. This had some local success but only sold about 500 copies.

In May of 1963, at seventeen, even before high school was done, he married Jennifer Lee Barton and, as these things will happen, soon a baby was on the way. Dana Scott Meisner was born in November of that same year. Randy felt he needed to make a living, so he dropped out of high school and devoted his entire time to his music.

Randy and Jennifer would be married for eighteen years and have two more children, Heather Leigh and Eric Shane Meisner, who, since they were both born in May of 1970, were probably twins.

Randy played with several different bands and then joined a group called the Soul Survivors. I am pretty sure this is not the same group who recorded the hit "Expressway to Your Heart" in 1967. Randy's group travelled to California where everyone was migrating in the late

Sixties and early Seventies and changed their name to the Poor, which is what they became as the group didn't really go anywhere.

When the Poor feel apart, Randy auditioned to be part of a new band that Richie Furay and Jim Messina were putting together which would be called Poco. Furay and Messina had both come from Buffalo Springfield. You almost need a roadmap to keep track of the movement of people during this time period as bands came and went and people moved from one band to another.

Randy recorded with Poco for their first album, *Pickin' Up the Pieces* in 1969 and then was asked to leave the band when he had a disagreement over studio techniques and album sound and the fact that Furay and Messina wouldn't let any of the other band members be involved in the final production of the album. They went so far as to edit out Randy's vocals and replaced them with another singer and then replaced his picture on the album cover with that of a dog. If you look at the album cover today, there's the dog. That's the spot Randy would have held. Naturally, Randy was very upset.

About this same time, Rick Nelson was putting together a new band called the Stone Canyon Band and wanted a sound which was much like Poco. One night when Poco was playing at a local club, Nelson happened to catch the act and really liked the way Randy played. When Rick Nelson heard that Randy was back on the market, he asked him to join the Stone Canyon Band. Randy did and played with Rick Nelson off and on until about 1971 when he decided he had had enough and left the band. He wanted to get back to his family in Nebraska. He can be heard on several Rick Nelson records during this time period but was not a part of the *Garden Party* album which put Rick Nelson back on the charts.

Thinking he was destined to be a wannabe in the music world, Randy returned home to Nebraska for a while to re-group and try to decide what to do. He had left his wife, Jennifer, in Nebraska for all these years, and she was growing tired of it. He got a job at a local John Deere tractor store and settled down to regular domestic life. However, it was not to last very long.

Soon, he got a call from John Boyton, who had been Rick Nelson's manager. He was assembling some musicians to act as a backup band for Linda Ronstadt. Randy knew of Glenn Frey and Don Henley. This was too good an opportunity to pass up so back to L.A. he went to get together with the other guys and make history.

5-BERNIE LEADON

Bernard Mathew Leadon III (known as Bernie) was born July 19, 1947 in Minneapolis, Minnesota to Dr. Bernard Leadon, Jr. and Ann Teresa Sweetser Leadon. Unlike a lot of musicians, he did not come from poverty. His father was an aerospace engineer and probably earned a pretty good salary, but they did tend to move a lot because of his job. Bernie came from a Catholic upbringing and was one of ten children.

The family was a musical family, like many others, and Bernie became interested in several different instruments from a young age. He would become quite proficient on the 5-string banjo, the mandolin, and the acoustic guitar. Most of his siblings turned out to be musical. His brother Mark and his sister Monica later formed the Leadon Family Band. Another brother, Tom Leadon, played with Tom Petty at one time. (In a piece of news unrelated to Bernie that I find interesting, his sister Monica ran for Mayor of Gainesville, Florida in 2010. She did not win.)

When he was a teenager, in the early Sixties, the family moved yet again, this time to San Diego, California. There, Bernie met two other guys who were interested in country and bluegrass music: Ed Douglas and Larry Murray. They formed a bluegrass band called "The Scottsville Squirrel Barkers." This band is important not just because of Bernie but because one of the founding members was Chris Hillman, who was later to be a founding member of the Byrds. Now, the Byrds did not last long and only had eight or so chart hits, but they are truly one of the Legends of Rock & Roll and will, most likely, be the subject of a future book in this series.

Hillman also was part of the Flying Burrito Brothers and is the Hillman in the Souther, Hillman, Furay Band, both great bands of the late Sixties in California.

The Scottsville Squirrel Barkers only recorded one album and didn't see much success. They disbanded in 1963. That same year, the Leadon family moved once again, this time to Gainesville, Florida where I think they stayed. Father Bernard got a more permanent job teaching at the University of Florida and Bernie continued with high school. Gainesville must be a hot bed of musical activity. There, Bernie met Don Felder who had a band of his own and would be a future Eagle. Stephen Stills of Crosby, Stills & Nash lived there for a time as did Tom Petty.

In 1967, after, I assume, Bernie graduated from high school; he got a call from former band mate Larry Murray who was putting together a band in Los Angeles called, "Hearts & Flowers." He convinced Bernie to come to California to play with the band. Hearts & Flowers would stay together for about two years recording two albums, neither of which did very much, but they are really valuable today if you can find them.

There are several Hearts & Flowers videos on YouTube (search for "hearts and flowers band") and you can get a real sense of the music of the late Sixties. In my opinion, it is really good stuff. The group, discouraged at the lack of sales, disbanded in 1968. Bernie had other friends in Los Angeles, and he hooked up with Doug Dillard and ex-Byrds member Gene Clark and became part of the new band Dillard & Clark.

He recorded with Dillard & Clark on two albums before the group disbanded. The first of the two, *The Fantastic Expedition of Dillard & Clark* released in 1968 is credited for being one of the masterpieces of the country rock genre of music. Bernie can be heard singing backgrounds on the album. In the second album, *Through the Morning, Through the Night*, Bernie plays but does not sing.

For the purposes of this discussion, the song I consider most important on the *Fantastic Expedition* album is "Train Leaves Here This Morning" which Bernie co-wrote and is included on the very first Eagles album with Bernie singing lead. Stop right now and go listen to it. The harmonies are wonderful. It became somewhat of a signature song for Bernie and is a great song.

Bernie left Dillard & Clark after the second album and re-united with his friend Chris Hillman, who had started yet another great band called The Flying Burrito Brothers. Hillman had joined together with Gram Parsons, who was also an ex-Byrd, to form the band and asked Bernie to join. Once again, Bernie played on two albums before leaving the band. *Burrito Deluxe* was released in 1970. Bernie is shown as co-writer on four of the songs on the album. *Deluxe* would be the last album by the group to include Gram Parsons before he was fired from the group. A song from this album, "Wild Horses" was written by Rolling Stones members Mick Jagger and Keith Richard but wasn't recorded by the Stones until a year later.

The second album by the Burrito Brothers was the self-titled *The Flying Burrito Brothers* but wasn't that successful commercially. Bernie was tired of being with bands that didn't make any money, so he quit the Brothers when he got the opportunity to play with three guys he had met the summer before when he moonlighted by playing in Linda Ronstadt's backup band. This time he got it right. This would be the defining moment of his career.

6-Becoming a Super Group

I mentioned before that we can thank Linda Ronstadt for the very existence of the Eagles. We also have to thank a man named John Boylan who was Ronstadt's manager at the time. Boylan is the man who hired each of the guys to be Ronstadt's backup band and literally brought them together so that they realized that the sum was greater than the parts.

Doug Weston's Troubadour was the place to go in Hollywood. Don called it the center of the musical universe. More stars than you can count have had their start at the Troubadour. On Monday nights, they held an open-mike night that they called "Hoot Night" and anyone could get up and sing. This is where Linda Ronstadt sang and created her backup band.

Boylan was looking for guys that would go on the road with Ronstadt and be her back-up band. He hired Glenn first for $250 a week and since that was more than he was making at the moment, Glenn took the job. Next, Don was added. Ronstadt had heard him play in Shiloh and Glenn and he were friends, so Glenn asked Don if he would like to join the group.

Boylan had the idea of putting together a super group of the best of the best to back up Linda Ronstadt, but Glenn and Don talked it over and they said to each other I would just rather be in a group with you. Why be in a backup band when you can be in your own band? They approached Linda and told her how much they appreciated the help she had given them, but they would rather create their own band. Linda was, amazingly enough, fine with it. She and Boylan both agreed that this was a great idea, and they supported them completely.

Linda knew this great banjo and guitar player named Bernie Leadon, and Glenn had met a guy named Randy Meisner and so they each approached them both and asked if they would like to be in a new band. They liked Randy because he could sing high and was a great bass guitar player. Therefore, the four got together and went to David Geffen who was owner of Asylum Records. Asylum was the place to be in the Seventies. All of the up and coming California groups recorded for Asylum including Jackson Browne.

Since Glenn and Don knew Browne, they asked him to get them an appointment with Geffen. They literally marched into his office and said sign us up. Here were four guys. They were cocky and sure of themselves, and Geffen was impressed. Furthermore, they didn't even have a name, yet.

Geffen told them they weren't ready to record yet. They needed to play together and write more songs. In the Seventies, you didn't start your career by covering other people's songs; you needed to write them yourself. They had to have an original sound and write original songs, so Geffen sent them to the boondocks: Aspen, Colorado. There, they played a small club and worked together and played together and, in general, learned how to be a band.

They really wanted to record an album, so they asked Glyn Johns to be their producer. Johns was a British producer who had been involved with the Rolling Stones, Led Zeppelin, and the Who. Johns came to Aspen to hear the band and was not impressed. He called them "confused." He was about to walk away when he thought maybe they'll do better in a studio where we have a controlled environment, so they went to Hollywood and played for him in a recording studio. Johns was still not that impressed. He suggested they take a break and during the break Glenn, Randy, and Bernie started to harmonize on a verse of an old song called "Silver Dagger." The harmonies were so wonderful that Johns stopped in his tracks and said, "That's what I'm been listening for!" He was in. They had a producer.

There was a catch, however. Johns, being British, didn't want to record in the United States, so he packed the guys off to London for their first recording session. They recorded at the Olympic Studios where such greats as The Beatles and Led Zeppelin had recorded plus many more. Johns was a task master. He didn't allow drinking or drugs in the studio. He required the artists to work and did not put up with any foolishness.

The inspiration for the cover of the first album came from a trip the guys made to the desert one night. There were seven in the group and after the Troubadour closed one night, they drove to Joshua Tree in the Mohave Desert. They took along peyote buttons to experience the desert as fully as possible (Native Americans ate peyote buttons when they went on a spiritual quest or in an effort to communicate with their spirit animals.)

The guys really just wanted to get high. They stopped at a campsite, built a fire, and everyone was eating a button. It was very surreal. Bernie says he thinks they got higher that night than they had ever gotten before. Glenn gets up during this time and needs to go pee in the bushes, so he is doing his business and the guys start yelling, "Eagle" and above them in the air is an eagle with his wings at full span soaring over them. That image of the eagle is on the cover of their first album and the image on the cover is of that desert trip.

And while I can't prove it, I'd like to think that it was that night in the desert that created the name "Eagles." Glenn later said that the name of the band was "Eagles" not "The Eagles." There is no "The" in their name.

7-"EAGLES" (THE ALBUM)

On June 22, 1972, Eagles released their first album, the self-titled *Eagles*. The album reached number twenty two on the album chart. The album is listed as number 374 of the 500 Greatest Albums of All Time from Rolling Stone magazine. The album produced three Top 40 hits, all of which are classic Eagles songs. Their first single on May 1, 1972 was "Take It Easy." The song was written by Jackson Browne, but he had gotten as far as the second verse and he was stuck. He wrote "I was standing on a corner in Winslow, Arizona" and couldn't come up with the next line. Glenn Frey, being Browne's friend, said let me take a stab at it, so Glenn followed it with "What a fine sight to see/it's a girl, my Lord, in a flat-bed Ford slowing down to take a look at me."

Therefore, writing credit to "Take It Easy" goes to both Browne and Glenn. I was in college when this song came out. I was your typical overweight dork that women never looked at. They really shouldn't have anyway, since I was married by this time. I remember hearing this song and thinking, '*Wow, I wish that would happen to me just once.*' Of course, it never did, it was just a song, but it held great meaning for me. The song reached number twelve on the Billboard Top 40 which was a good showing for a new and unknown band. It is listed on the 500 songs that shaped rock and roll which was published by *Rolling Stone* magazine.

There is a bronze statue on a corner in front of a store in Winslow, Arizona. Above the statue is a sign reading "Standing on a corner." The statue shows a man carrying a guitar. It is a fitting honor to an American band.

Their second song from the *Eagles* album was "Witchy Woman" which was written by Bernie Leadon and Don Henley. Bernie had written the music for the song back when he was with the Flying

Burrito Brothers, but no one had recorded it. Don heard the music, thought it would make a great Eagles song, and put words to the music. "Witchy Woman" peaked at number nine on the Top 40.

There's a lot of speculation as to who the witchy woman was intended to be, but Don says it refers to Zelda Fitzgerald, the wife of F. Scott Fitzgerald. In the novel, "The Great Gatsby", the character of Dixie Buchanan (played by Carey Mulligan in the new movie) is based upon Zelda. Zelda spent some time in a mental institution and the line in the song, "She drove herself to madness with the silver spoon" refers to that and the drugs she would take.

After "Witchy Woman", they released "Peaceful Easy Feeling" which was written by Jack Tempchin. The song is meant to take you into the peace of the desert where you can relax and get high. The song peaked at number twenty two on the Top 40 but is known today as one of the Eagles' most famous songs.

Both "Peaceful Easy Feeling" and "Take It Easy" were later said to be a reaction to the turmoil of the Sixties. I'm not sure the guys had that specifically in mind when they wrote them but after the Vietnam War and Watergate, the country was a mess. The Eagles slowed things down and told everyone that everything was going to be all right. Just take it easy and be at peace. Things will work out.

8-"DESPERADO"

Their second album was *Desperado*. The album was released on April 17, 1973 and didn't do quite as well as the first album peaking at number forty one on the album charts. Glenn Frey says, "It bombed"; however, it produced two Eagles' classics.

This album is significant, though, for the reason that it was with "Desperado" that Don and Glenn began to collaborate on writing their songs. Almost every song on the album has the writing credit given to Henley/Frey. It reminds me of the Lennon/McCartney team when The Beatles were together.

The album is called a "concept" album. It's really about cowboys and outlaws. Specifically, it's about the Dalton Gang in the old west. The Dalton Gang was famous in that they terrorized the west for about two years from 1890 until 1892. They were finally brought down in Coffeyville, Kansas when they attempted to rob two banks at the same time.

I especially remember two songs from *Desperado*. The first is "Tequila Sunrise" which is a beautiful song that features the harmonies of the four. The song did not make the Top 40; however, it did peak at number sixty four. It has since become one of the most requested songs by Eagles' fans.

The other song that I remember was never a single at all. The title song "Desperado" is a great song and even though it doesn't appear on the charts, I remember it well from the Seventies and later. The song was written by the Henley/Frey team and is listed at number 494 on *Rolling Stone* magazine's 500 Greatest Songs of All Time. "Desperado" is well known as an Eagles' classic.

I remember an unusual event which happened in 1980. I had to go back through Google listings to find the news story, but I did find it, and I know it happened. In New York, a truck driver took a disc jockey hostage at a radio station, WPLJ-FM, and demanded that the DJ play the song "Desperado." The way I remember it, it was played several times before the police broke in and arrested the guy but in reality, he only made the DJ play the song once. He wanted to borrow $2,500 from the Eagles for some problem he was having. He held the DJ at gunpoint for about 90 minutes before peacefully surrendering to the police. It's funny, the things you remember.

The other song that was released as a single was "Outlaw Man." This song did a little better than "Tequila Sunrise" and peaked at number fifty nine on the charts, not making the Top 40. I have to admit that I do not remember this song from the Seventies at all. It may be that I was graduating from college about that time and not paying attention, but I suspect it wasn't played as much as their other hits.

You can find a video on YouTube of "Outlaw Man" that has an awesome introduction on the banjo by Bernie Leadon. That alone makes it worth listening to the song.

9-"On the Border"

The guys were very unhappy with the sound of *Desperado* and blamed Johns for it, so, they started looking for a new producer. They found him in Bill Szymczyk (pronounced "Simzik".) Szymczyk had had no musical background when he entered the business. He had been in the military and had learned about electronics and found that he made a pretty good recording engineer. One day, he thought to himself, '*I think I can produce a record just as good as the people I'm working for*', so he became a producer.

The guys wanted Eagles to have a more hard rock sound. They didn't think the country-rock sound was working for them. They had heard that Szymczyk had produced an album for Joe Walsh which was definitely a rock album and, so they arranged a meeting.

In the meeting, they asked him two things: will you let us control the sound of the recordings and can we put a separate mike on each drum so that we can control the mix better? Szymczyk said yes to both, and they had themselves a new producer.

Bernie was beginning to have doubts about his place in the band. Bernie was really good at the country-rock sound but couldn't, or didn't want to, play rock. Glenn could play rock but wasn't good at playing the more country style. They decided they needed another guitarist.

Bernie had a friend who lived back east named Don Felder who happened to be in California for another matter. They called up Don and asked him to come and jam with them one night, so Don came over and the five of them jammed. Don did not realize that he was in the middle of an audition. Apparently, they liked what they heard because a day or so after he had returned back home, Glenn called him and asked him if he'd like to a part of Eagles. He said, "Are you kidding? Of course!" (I just made up the "are you kidding" part, but that is what I would have said.)

Now the four Eagles were five.

10-DON FELDER

Donald William Felder was born September 21, 1947 in Gainesville, Florida, the son of Charles "Nolan" Felder and Doris Brigman. Like so many performers who grew up in the south, his family was poor, and Don had to work for what he got. I would never have guessed that Gainesville was the home of so many famous people, and Don knew most of them.

His father was a mechanic and worked at a factory not far from their house. Don had one older brother, Jerry, who was five years older than he. We almost lost Don as a guitar player when he was four-years-old. He fell out of a tree that he had been told not to climb in the first place and fractured his left arm. The doctor told him it was broke beyond repair, and he would never be able to do anything with the arm. His mother thought otherwise.

She would fill a bucket with sand and have him carry it to strengthen his arm. After a couple of years of exercise, it was almost as good as new. Without the attention of his mother, he might never have been able to play.

Breaking his arm was bad enough but when he was five, he contracted polio. Polio was a dangerous disease in the Fifties but luckily for Don the Sulk vaccine had just been invented, and he was able to get a dose. He spent four months in the polio ward of his local hospital, but he came out of it OK.

His interest in music began like a lot of other people. Like Randy Meisner, he first saw Elvis Presley on *Ed Sullivan* and decided he wanted to make music. He traded six cherry bombs (fire crackers) with another kid for a simple guitar when he was ten-years-old. Then, he proceeded to teach himself to play. He says he practiced with that simple first guitar until his fingers bled.

When he was eleven, a friend of his father sold him a Fender Musicmaker guitar. It was a real step up. Using this new guitar, Don performed in public for the first time. At a local theater, they would show a Saturday morning movie and afterwards, they would hold a sort of amateur hour. Don was very nervous, but he played and to his amazement, they didn't boo him.

His first band in high school was called, "The Continentals" and included several of his friends. You know I love to name drop, so it won't surprise you to find out that one of the members of his band was Stephen Stills. He was fifteen at the time. I'm not sure if there is anyone who has not heard of Crosby, Stills, & Nash, one of the greatest bands in rock and roll history and certainly a subject of a future Legends of Rock & Roll book. Don says Stills just showed up one day and started playing with them and then one day, he was just gone. He left, and no one knew where he went.

Don also got to meet a very young Tom Petty, called Tommy Petty, when he got a job at a local music store to teach people how to play the guitar. As you probably know, Tom Petty became one of the biggest stars of the Eighties. Gainesville, Florida was a hot bed of future stars in the Sixties.

In 1963, Don met the man who would have more impact on his life than any other outside his family: Bernie Leadon. I mentioned before that Bernie had moved to Gainesville, and he stopped by the music store to ask the owner who was the best guitarist in Gainesville. The owner told him, Don Felder. Bernie sought him out and the two became lifelong friends. Bernie joined the Continentals which changed its name to the Maundy Quintet. They thought the name sounded British because The Beatles were just becoming big.

The Maundy Quintet actually cut a record, and you can hear it on YouTube. If you want to hear some early Don Felder/Bernie Leadon, go check it out.

After graduating from high school in 1966, the Maundy Quintet broke up. Bernie headed for California and Don went to New York and joined a band named Flow. He stayed with Flow until about 1970. They had recorded one album and then broke up so, in 1970, Don moved to Boston. All this time, he was getting better and better on the guitar, trying out new ideas, and becoming more proficient in his craft.

In 1972, Don moved to California and got a job playing with David Blue who was a musician trying to make a name in the industry. The only thing I can find that Blue did that we might remember was he wrote the song "Outlaw Man" for the Eagles. Blue and Don and his band toured with Crosby and Nash during 1972. One day, Don got called by Bernie Leadon to come play on a recording session for their song "Good Day in Hell." He didn't know it was an audition. The next day, Glenn called and we are back to the point we started.

The band called Don Felder, "Fingers Felder" because of the way he played the guitar.

11-Girls, Drugs, and Rock & Roll

It was the Seventies. If you think the Sixties was the drug decade, I think the Seventies was worse. The band members had two things on their minds, maybe three: girls, drugs, and music. That was their life. After each concert, they had a party they called the third encore. During the concert, the guys would do two encores for the crowd. Then the party or "the third encore" would start back stage and the girls would come and the drugs would be handed out and everyone would get stoned and hook up with someone. After all, this is rock and roll and the main reason most guys got into rock and roll was for the girls and the drugs and the music.

I love this story. The group really liked to gamble. They would get together among themselves and play poker whenever they could. One day, they decided to fly down to the Bahamas to do some real gambling at the casinos down there. Two or three of them packed drugs in their clothing and taped it to their body to smuggle it into the Bahamas. When they reached customs, they were immediately taken aside to be searched. Glenn says he could just picture spending the next five years in a Bahaman jail, but once they got them into a room to do the searching, Irving Azoff, who was their manager at the time, took one of the customs guys aside and whispered something in his ear. The next thing they knew, they were all being released and were on their way to a great vacation. To this day, Azoff has never revealed what he said to the customs man, but everyone was sure glad he did.

There were two big hits from the "On the Border" album. "Already Gone" was released April 19, 1974. It was written by Jack Tempchin and Robb Strandlund. Although it is a song that is well known among Eagle fans, it only got to number thirty two on the Top 40. I think that may be because Eagles were becoming an album band and FM radio was developing stations that specialized in album cuts, deemphasizing the singles. The Top 40 was not as important as it was in the Fifties and Sixties.

In April of 1974, an event occurred in California which Eagles were a part. Called "California Jam" this was the musical event of the year. Called the "Woodstock of the West Coast," it included many of the great bands from the early Seventies. It brought Eagles to the attention of many people that had not heard them before. Some of the concert was telecast on ABC television. There were over 300,000 people in Ontario, California and some of the bands that played were Deep Purple, Black Sabbath, Emerson Lake & Palmer, and other great performers.

They followed up "Already Gone" in March of 1975 with "Best of My Love" which became their first number one song seemly negating what I said in the previous paragraph about albums. "Best of My Love" was written by Don Henley, Glenn Frey, and his old friend J.D. Souther. Don Henley sang lead on the song which he was doing more and more. "Best of My Love" the song was done earlier by John Lees and Tanya Tucker but neither version charted. Yvonne Elliman recorded it after Eagles, but her version did not chart either. In case you're thinking about the Emotions version of "Best of My Love", that was also a number one song in 1977, but it is an entirely different song. The Emotions did a Disco-sounding song with the same name.

12-"One of These Nights"

In mid-1975 (June), the group released its fourth studio album, *One of These Nights*. This would be the first of four number one albums in a row for the group. People were starting to call them a super group. Their first single from the album was the title track and like their last hit, it went to number one. The song was written by the Frey/Henley team as usual and again Don Henley sings lead on the song with Randy Meisner doing what they call high harmony in the background. According to Glenn, the song is about putting things off. One of these nights we're going to get around to fulfilling our dream, whatever it may be. Glenn also has said that this is his overall favorite Eagles song.

The second single from the album was "Lyin' Eyes." It reached number two on the charts. This is one of my favorite Eagles songs. I know just what the girl is going through in the song. The guys say that the inspiration for the song came from them watching young girls come to their shows with older men. Glenn said you could look at them and tell that they had lying eyes. In the song, the girl lies to her older husband and goes off to be with a younger man. The older guy has cold hands, so I understand the problem. It happens when you get older and your circulation slows down. I think the moral here is, stick to people your own age.

"Lyin' Eyes" won them their first Grammy Award for Best Pop Vocal Performance by a Group and was nominated for Record of the Year in 1975. It also appears on the soundtrack of the movie *Urban Cowboy*, a 1980 movie.

Up until now, almost all of the leads had been sung by either Glenn Frey or Don Henley. Randy Meisner could sing lead also. He had a higher pitched voice and sounded really good as a lead singer but had never been given the chance. For their third hit from the album, "Take It to the Limit," they turned the lead over to Randy. Randy also helped write the song, so you could say it was made for him. The song reached number four on the Top 40 and was the first single of their career to go gold. It would, however, be the only song on which Randy sang lead. It was also the last single that featured Bernie Leadon on guitar.

In fact, in December of 1975, Bernie had had enough. He was a country guitar player, and the group was moving more and more toward rock. Bernie was tired of the touring and the constant pressure that the band was under. He was also tired of the drugs which everyone in the band was just assumed to participate. One night, Bernie cracked. The breaking point was reached one day when the group was backstage at the Orange Bowl in Miami. Bernie calmly got up and poured a beer over the head of Glenn Frey. To this day, Bernie says he doesn't know why he did it. He was not trying to be disrespectful; he had just reached his limit.

About this same time, Irving Azoff was managing a fellow by the name of Joe Walsh. Joe was something of a wild man. He had already had a pretty good career and was doing well on his own, but the group needed a replacement for Bernie. They asked Joe if he'd like to join the band.

They tried him out by bringing him on stage in a big box and then had him jump out of it like a girl jumps out of a cake and then he would launch into "Rocky Mountain Way," one of his solo hits. Joe had the effect of changing their sound when he joined Eagles. They were now moving more toward a real rock band.

13-JOE WALSH

Joseph Fidler was born November 20, 1947 in Wichita, Kansas. His birth father's last name was Fidler, but his mother didn't stay with him very long, if they were married at all. At the age of five, Joe was officially adopted by his stepfather, whose name was Walsh and he took Fidler as his middle name, legally becoming Joseph Fidler Walsh.

It appears that Joe had at least two brothers, Mark and Frank. Mark is a musician as well and is active in New Jersey. It's difficult to find information on Frank, other than I'm pretty sure he exists. There is no information on other siblings Joe might have.

The family moved around a lot when Joe was younger. They spent time first in Columbus, Ohio and then when Joe was eleven, they moved to New York City. Feeling that the big city was a bad influence on Joe, when he was fourteen, they next moved to Montclair, New Jersey. Joe finished high school in Montclair, graduating in the class of 1965.

Joe comes about his musical ability naturally since his mother was a classical pianist. During high school, he joined the band and at first played the clarinet and oboe. Joe says he liked to be the center of attention and the entire band tunes up to the sound of the oboe, so they all had to listen to him.

However, as much as he liked attention, he also liked girls, and you can't get girls by playing the oboe, so he switched to the guitar. After High School, Joe attended Kent State University located in Kent, Ohio. He didn't finish, but he was involved with a couple of bands while he was there. One was called the G-Clefs and another called Measles. He was not there during the famous Kent State shooting in

1970 when four students were killed for protesting the war. It had a great impact upon him, however, as it did many people.

In January of 1968, he replaced Glen Schwartz as lead guitarist for the James Gang. The James Gang changed personnel frequently and by summer, they were down to just three members. Opening for Cream in Detroit, Michigan, they realized they liked the sound of a trio and so that was the way they stayed. Joe would stay with the James Gang until 1971 when he left to go solo. In a list of former members of the James Gang I found online, it lists 22 names and there were never more than four or five at a time and toward the end of the Sixties, there were just the three.

Joe has been married four or five times, it depends on who you read. His first wife was Stephanie. They were married in 1971 and divorced in 1978. They had one daughter, Emma Kristen, who was tragically killed in an automobile accident when she was three. Joe has written a song to Emma, "Song for Emma" which is included on a 1974 album called *So What*.

Although officially a solo act, Joe created his own band, Barnstorm, in 1972. They would record three albums over the next couple of years. The first, the self-titled *Barnstorm* did not make much of an impression, but the second album, *The Smoker You Drink, The Player You Get* was a breakthrough hit. The album made the Top 10, peaking at number six. This was due primarily to the single "Rocky Mountain Way" which was Joe's first big hit. It peaked at number 23 on the Top 40 singles chart. The song is credited to Joe Walsh, but the entire Barnstorm band plays on it.

Joe is credited for inventing something called "The Talkbox" which was a device he connected to his guitar, and he would sing through it and the sound would be a metallic sounding voice. Today, they use different devices to achieve that sound, but Joe was the first one to do it. Listen to "Rocky Mountain Way," you'll hear what I mean.

"Rocky Mountain Way" has an interesting genesis. Joe had moved to Colorado by this time and literally had the mountains in his back yard. He says he was out in his yard mowing the grass when he looked up and noticed just how beautiful the mountains were. He thought, the Rocky Mountain way is better than the way I had. Suddenly the words and the music to the song were in his head. He dropped the mower and ran into the house to write it down. Unfortunately, he forgot to turn off the lawn mower, so it kept running merrily on its way until it had cut through his yard and gone on into his neighbor's yard and mowed down half of the neighbor's garden. Joe felt bad about that. He said it was an expensive lesson.

In 1974, he released another solo album, *So What*. Then, in 1975, he replaced Bernie Leadon as a member of Eagles. And we have come full circle again.

14-"Hotel California"

You almost need a scorecard to keep up with the changing personnel in the band. Bernie was now gone with Joe Walsh taking his place. "Rocky Mountain Way" became a staple of an Eagles concert as they added in the songs that Joe had done before he joined the group. Before getting to their next studio album, I must mention their first album of greatest hits. Simply called, *Their Greatest Hits 1971–1975*, it was released in early 1976 and some say that it is the bestselling album of all time. Actually, I'm not sure if that is true. If you Google "Bestselling album of all time" every website you go to lists a different answer. I tend to believe the Recording Industry Association of America (RIAA) which places it in a tie with Michael Jackson's *Thriller* at sales of 29 Million, but I think Michael Jackson has a slight edge.

The next Eagles studio album came out on December 8, 1976 and was the first to feature Joe Walsh. *Hotel California* would become a blockbuster hit and truly establish the group as a super group. The album became their highest selling studio album and was another number one on the album charts. The album is ranked number 37 on Rolling Stone magazine's list of the 500 Greatest Albums of All Time.

The album won two Grammys in 1978, one for Record of the Year (which actually went to the producer, Bill Szymczyk) and one for their first single from the album "New Kid in Town" which won for Best Arrangement for Voices.

The cover of the album is a photograph of the Beverly Hills Hotel which was taken by David Alexander. Don Henley says that *Hotel California* is a concept album in much the same way as *Desperado* was. Only instead of a cowboy album, this one was urban. It is meant to represent the materialism and decadence of the world we live in.

The album was released in 1976 which was the bicentennial of our country. It portrays just how far we have fallen in 200 years. Don Henley has said, "It's a fine line between the American Dream and the American Nightmare". You may agree or disagree.

The first single from the album was their third number one song on the Billboard Top 40 charts. "New Kid in Town" was actually released the day before the album, on December 7, 1976 and by Christmas day, it was number one. It also went to number twenty in the United Kingdom.

The song is about things that are temporary and fleeting, like love can be, but they are really talking about themselves. The Eagles were hot in 1977 but how long would it last? Every rock star knows that fame is temporary and maybe tomorrow someone new will come along, and you will be forgotten. You're still there, but no one is paying attention to you. Now, there's a new kid in town.

Next they released the title song "Hotel California" in February of 1977. The song is considered by many to be one of the greatest rock songs of all time; it was ranked number 49 on *Rolling Stone*'s list of The 500 Greatest Songs of All Time.

Continuing on the theme of the entire album, the single is about a hotel that seems inviting and welcoming but turns out to be a trap. Don Henley says it represents the hedonism and greed that was rampant in the music industry in the late Seventies. The song is about the dark underbelly of the American Dream. Henley and Frey wrote most of the words, but the music came from Don Felder who had written it as an instrumental.

The single "Hotel California" also peaked at number one and became their fourth number one. Writing credit goes to three this time: Don Felder, Glenn Frey, and Don Henley. Henley sings lead and the song ends with some of my favorite words in a song: "You can check out anytime you like/but you can never leave." The song then concludes with over a minute and a half of the guitar styling of Felder and Walsh. This instrumental ending is one of the most famous in rock history and probably responsible for the fame of this single. I have heard it said that Don Felder and Joe Walsh complemented each other perfectly on guitars. They are called "the bookends of the band."

The third and final single from the album was "Life in the Fast Lane," a more upbeat rocking song that features a Joe Walsh riff in the middle. Another song about excess, this song was written by Walsh, Frey, and Henley. The guitar intro and the riff in the middle and the outgoing guitar at the end are all Joe Walsh.

The song reached number eleven on the Top 40. It has been covered by several other performers, and Joe plays it during solo tours that he still does to this day.

15-TRASHING HOTELS

Sounds like a good name for an album but no, this is about the reputation the guys got in the late Seventies for literally destroying hotel rooms that they stayed in on tours. Don Henley says there are hotels now that won't let them stay there because of the damage they did.

You may have heard of Joe Walsh and his chainsaw which he received as a Christmas present from Don Henley. Yes, Joe would travel with a chainsaw and when he saw a wall that he felt needed a door in it so he could get into the next room he cut his own door right in the wall. Joe was called the American king of room trash. I've also heard him called "The Clown Prince of Rock." Joe brought a lot of humor to the group who all tended to be very serious about their work. Sometimes that was appreciated and sometimes, it wasn't.

There's a famous story that occurred in Chicago at the Astor Towers which is a pretty nice place. There's a knock at the door and in walks John Bulushi, the actor. Bulushi wanted to take Joe to a fancy restaurant so they appeared at the door of one of Chicago's finest eating establishments, but the maître de wouldn't let them in because they were wearing jeans, so Bulushi took the two of them to an alley and spray painted their jeans black. Well, they got into the restaurant but when they got up from their chairs, the seats of the chairs were black with paint. These were probably $500 chairs and so they ran.

That same night, Joe and John Bulushi set out to break the record for room trashing. They did $28,000 worth of damage to the hotel room before they were done.

They felt that to be respected as true rock stars, they had to be "bad boys," so they set about to live up to that reputation.

16-Discord Among the Ranks

A song which did end up on the *Hotel California* album was largely responsible for Don Felder leaving the group. "Victim of Love" was the final cut on the A-side of the album, and Don Felder came up with the genesis of the guitar work that is heard on this song. The problem was, Felder wanted to sing the song. After Henley and Frey fleshed out the song, they tried to record it with Don Felder doing the lead vocals, but Felder wasn't a singer. He was a great guitar player but not a singer.

I read they tried dozens of times to get a good recording with Felder as vocalist, but it just did not come up to the "band's standards," so Irving Azoff, their manager, took Felder out to lunch one day and while they were gone, Don Henley recorded his vocals over the top of Felder's, thus cutting his voice out of the song. While Felder was not happy about this, he did admit it sounded better with Henley singing it.

Another problem was Randy Meisner. Randy had really only been lead singer on one song for the Eagles, "Take It to the Limit." It had high notes, and Randy was having trouble reaching them some nights. I try to imagine what it would be like to go out in front of a crowd every night and sing the same songs over and over again for years on end…

Well, Randy was tired of "Take It to the Limit." He didn't want to do the song any more. Glenn tried to talk to him and convince him that the fans really liked that song and wanted to hear it. They usually did the song as an encore and one night, it all came to a head. Randy refused to go on and do the song. The guys almost came to blows as Glenn Frey and Don Henley tried to reason with Randy and convince him to sing, but he would not do it. In fairness to Randy, he had spent much of the previous year very sick. He suffered from stomach ulcers and had contacted the flu a time or two. I think life on the road was just getting too difficult for him.

And just like that: Randy was out. It's not clear if he was fired or if he just quit, but Randy Meisner, one of the founding members of the band Eagles, was now gone. It was 1977.

Glenn says there was never any question about who would replace Randy. They called an old friend who the guys knew from the Sixties. When Randy Meisner had left the band Poco, the man who replaced him was Timothy B. Schmit. Now, Timothy would be the man who replaced him in the Eagles.

17-Timothy B Schmit

Timothy Bruce Schmit was born October 30, 1947 in Oakland, California, the son of Danny and Janey Schmit. His father, Danny Schmit, was a vacuum cleaner salesman by day and a musician by night, so Timothy came by his talent honestly, and I'm sure it was a big boost to his learning to play and sing. Right after he was born, the family (including at least one brother) lived in a trailer that they pulled all over California as father Danny went from gig to gig.

When Timothy was about seven, they settled in Sacramento. Being musically minded right from the start, Timothy first took tap dancing lessons and then took up the violin, trombone, and finally the guitar. If you want to make it big in music, start young and have a band in high school. That seems to be the pattern that works. Timothy got together with some friends and created a band called Tim, Tom, & Ron. This was the middle of the folk era in the United States and so that is what they played.

In 1962 or so, surfing music became the rage and so you go where the audience is; thus, they changed their name to the Contenders and played surfing music just like the Beach Boys. In 1964, The Beatles hit America like a bomb and the Mersey Beat was the thing to do, so the guys let their hair grow long, and they tried to imitate The Beatles. Oh and that necessitated another name change, so they became the New Breed. This band finally began to attract some attention. They actually got to open for some big names like Sonny & Cher and Herman's Hermits.

After high school, Timothy started college at Sacramento State College as a psychology major. I don't think he thought you could make a living playing the guitar. The New Breed morphed back into what they started with: a folk style band and they now called themselves Glad. Glad recorded one album before breaking up.

Unlike the other guys in the band, Timothy already lived in California, so he was familiar with the scene there. Glad only recorded one album, *Feelin' Glad.* It was released in 1968 on ABC Records, but it didn't sell. It's amazing, but you can still get the album on Amazon, probably because of the later fame of Timothy B Schmit.

Glad didn't last long and broke up after the failure of the album. Timothy happened to run into Richie Furay, who was a founder of Buffalo Springfield. Furay was putting together a new band which he called Pogo. The name Pogo was currently the name of a comic strip that ran nationwide. Walt Kelly, the cartoonist who owned Pogo, sued Furay for using the name and so Furay changed the name of the band to Poco. Furay asked Timothy to audition for the bass guitar position in Poco.

Timothy did but another guitarist also auditioned for that position in the band: a guy named Randy Meisner, and Randy got the job. As we know from previous chapters on Randy Meisner, he didn't stay with Poco very long. He is heard on their first album but given no credit after he left the band.

So Furay called Timothy and asked him if he still wanted the job. Absolutely he did and so Timothy B Schmit became a member of Poco. I've read that Poco did some great work in the next seven years but never really connected with the public, so they weren't that successful commercially.

Timothy was still playing with Poco when Glenn Frey called him and asked him to join his band Eagles. It must have felt like he had just won the lottery. Poco had been around since the late Sixties but had never had a hit. In fact, it wasn't until Timothy left and they created a new lineup in 1979, that they had their first Top 40 hit. It might make you think Timothy was holding them back, but I don't think that's true. Maybe someday, I'll go into the details behind Poco.

18-"THE LONG RUN"

In 1977, the band went back to the studio for their next album, *The Long Run*. It took them two years to make the album and it would be the last studio album for the Eagles for nearly 28 years. It was finally released on September 24, 1979. It proved to be a letdown for some critics after the enormous success of *Hotel California,* but the fans still loved the Eagles, and the album was very successful commercially, selling over 7 million copies.

The album topped the charts in the United States, Australia, Canada, and Sweden. As was their pattern up until now, the album would produce three hit singles. The first was their fifth and last number one single, "Heartache Tonight."

"Heartache Tonight" was written by the Frey/Henley team along with help from J.D. Souther and Bob Seger. Yes, you read that right, Bob Seger helped write "Heartache Tonight" and he even sang background vocals on the record. The story is that J.D. Souther and Glenn Frey were together at Glenn's house (they were still friends) listening to Sam Cooke music and working on the song when they got stuck on the chorus, so Souther called Bob Seger on the phone and asked for his help. Seger sang them the chorus over the phone. He just created it on the spot. The record won the Grammy Award for Best Rock Performance by a Duo or Group with Vocal.

The second single from *The Long Run* was the title track, and it reached number eight on the charts. The song was again written by Frey/Henley, again with some help from Bob Seger. The song is a tribute to the longevity of the Frey/Henley team although by this time, cracks were beginning to form in the relationship.

The song was featured on an episode of *WKRP in Cincinnati*, the television show. Do you remember that show? Dr. Johnny Fever was a disk jockey and usually played whatever he wanted to play, much to the dismay of Andy Travis, the station manager. One day, Fever played, "The Long Run" on his show, and Travis was delighted to hear something up-to-date and not just oldies. *WKRP in Cincinnati* was a great show, one of my favorites.

The third and last single from *The Long Run* was "I Can't Tell You Why." This song also reached number eight on the charts. It was written by the Frey/Henley team, this time with help from Timothy B Schmit. Furthermore, this is the first Eagles song on which Timothy sings the lead vocals.

About this time, the group recorded a single which did not appear on any album. This was a Christmas record with "Please Come Home for Christmas" on one side and "Funky New Year" on the other. This was for the Christmas season of 1978 and "Please Come Home for Christmas" reached number eighteen on the Top 40 which was rare for a Christmas single in the late Seventies. Christmas music used to make the charts all the time in the Fifties and before and even a little into the Sixties, but by now, sales for holiday music usually just weren't strong enough to do the job.

In 1978, Glenn met his first wife, Janie Beggs, a Texas debutante. He decided that he wanted to settle down and so they started dating. They went together for five years before they finally decided to make it legal. They married in 1983, but by 1986, the magic had worn off, and they decided to divorce.

Also in 1978, Joe Walsh recorded an album without the rest of the guys in Eagles called "But Seriously, Folks." Although, this is listed as a solo album, all of the rest of the current Eagles band played with him on it. The album would reach number eight on the album chart. His second solo hit, "Life's Been Good" was the main single from this album. The song peaked at number twelve on the Top 40 and was his highest ranking song of his career as a soloist.

19-The Long Vacation

Contention was increasing among the ranks of the members of the band. Don Henley and Glenn Frey were still friends, but it was strained. Don Felder really disliked Glenn Frey and the two almost came to blows several times. It all came to a head on July 31, 1980 when they played Long Beach, California. Tempers were at a breaking point. These guys had been together almost ten years and, I think, were just tired of it. One of the band members called it "Long Day at Wrong Beach."

The guys started telling each other what they were going to do to them when the show was over. This was on stage in front of the audience. Don Felder said to Glenn Frey, "Only three more songs and then I'm going to kick your ass." During the song "Best of My Love," which, remember, is a ballad, they were both thinking, *'When this is over, I'm going to kill him.'*

When the concert was over, Don Felder ran off stage ahead of the rest of guys, took his guitar, and smashed it against the wall. Leaving the pieces behind, he jumped into his limo and drove away. That was, essentially, the end of the Eagles.

Glenn Frey says they were all type-A personalities, and each wanted to be top dog. That wasn't possible and so friction resulted. I'm just glad they lasted as long as they did.

The band was ready to break up right that night, but they still had a contract to Electra Records for one more live album based on the tour they had just finished. Even Frey and Henley would not be in the same studio with each other. They didn't even want to be in the same state, so Don Henley went to the east coast to work on the last album and Glen Frey stayed on the west coast and everything was delivered back and forth by Federal Express.

In November of 1980, *Eagles Live* was delivered to Electra in fulfillment of their contract. The liner notes just contained one sentence: "Thank you and goodnight." It seemed that the band was done.

There's one more song to talk about, however, and I believe it is one of their best. It came from the *Eagles Live* album and was "Seven Bridges Road." It is not an original Eagles song. It was written back in the mid-Sixties by a musician named Steve Young. Young recorded it in 1969, but the version that the world remembers is the one done by the Eagles.

The story of the song is that there was a road that led out of Montgomery, Alabama and proceeded out into the country where you could go to get high or just get away from the city and the road crossed seven bridges before getting to its destination. This was the inspiration of the song. The five part harmony that the guys sing when they recorded this song just brings goose bumps to my skin. It is such a beautiful song. It was recorded live in Santa Monica, California and was included on the live album. It reached number 21 on the charts and would be the last chart hit for the Eagles for fourteen years.

Glenn Frey would never admit that the Eagles had broken up. That term was never used. Glenn just said, "We are on a long vacation." The Eagles' last performance was July 31, 1980. They reunited on April 25, 1994 to play together for the first time in fourteen years

When someone asked Don Henley what it was like when the Eagles broke up – he said it was a horrible release.

20-The Solo Years of Don Henley

The guys really went their own ways after the breakup. They didn't want anything to do with one another for quite some time. Each started or revived a solo career. Some were more successful than others.

Of the five, Don Henley and Glenn Frey were probably the most successful as solo artists. Don's girlfriend at the time was Stevie Nicks of Fleetwood Mac fame, so the first thing he did was get together with her and record a duet called "Leather and Lace" which peaked at number six in the Top 40. His first solo album was *I Can't Stand Still* which went gold and peaked at number 46 on the album charts. The album produced three singles, but only one of them, "Dirty Laundry" (#3) reached the Top 40 charts. This was a very personal album for Don. The songs were mostly his comments on the world around him. "Dirty Laundry" was his comment on current politics and "Johnny Can't Read" criticized the public educational system.

In 1984, he followed up with *Building the Perfect Beast*. This album was even bigger than the first, peaking at number thirteen and selling three million copies. It spawned four singles, all of which reached the Top 40. First was "The Boys of Summer" (#5) which I enjoyed watching on MTV in the mid-Eighties. I remember it being one of our favorite videos. I had at first thought the song was about baseball, but it's not. It's more about summer love and the loss of innocence. Then there was an up tempo number "All She Wants to Do is Dance" (#9) and is another indictment of American culture: All we do is dance when there are much more important things to be concerned about. Two lesser hits also hit the Top 40, "Not Enough Love in the World" (#34) and "Sunset Grill (#22) finished out the album.

It wasn't until 1989 that he released his third album. *The End of the Innocence* (#6 – album charts) sold six million copies, doing much better than his first two solo albums.

The album kept up his criticism of American culture with the title song which reached number eight on the Top 40. The song was co-written by Bruce Hornsby and Hornsby is featured on the record.

Next was "The Last Worthless Evening" (#21) in October of 1989 which is rumored to be about Michelle Pfeiffer. Don was at a party in Hollywood when he spotted Pfeiffer across the room sitting with Jack Nicholson. He walked over and asked Pfeiffer if he could bum a cigarette. Without even looking at him or acknowledging his presence, she handed him a cigarette. Nicholson remarked "Well played, Henley" and Don walked away. That is said to be the genesis of the song. Lastly, "The Heart of the Matter" (#21) was released in 1989 but didn't chart until March of 1990.

His last single to chart was "Sometimes Love Just Ain't Enough" (#2) which he sang with Patty Smyth who was the former lead singer of Scandal which was kind of an alternative band in the Eighties. Don takes a back seat to Smyth in the song, but their harmonies are very nice. While Don gets credit on the record, it's basically Patty Smyth's song. It would be the last time Don Henley would chart as a solo artist.

21-The Solo Years of Glenn Frey

On his own, Glenn Frey hooked up with Jack Tempshin who had written several songs for the Eagles back in the Seventies. In 1982, Glenn released his first solo album, *No Fun Aloud* which gave the impression that Glenn was having fun with his music. The album did moderately well, peaking at number thirty two on the album charts and eventually going gold.

The album produced two weak singles, "I Found Somebody" (#32) and "The One That You Love" (#15) but did establish him as a serious performer in his own right. His second album cemented that feeling in the minds of his fans. *The Allnighter* was released in 1984 and peaked at number twenty two which was and still is his highest charting album. *The Allnighter* contains also two singles: "Sexy Girl" (#20) and "Smuggler's Blues" (#12).

Sandwiched between those two singles, Glenn recorded a song for the movie *Beverly Hills Cop* which starred Eddie Murphy. "The Heat is On" is a rousing up tempo song with a strong drum beating in the background. The song got extensive MTV air play as the video was shown frequently. This resulted in the song hitting number two on the Billboard Top 40. This made Glenn, officially, the highest charting ex-Eagle. Don Henley never did that well and neither did any of the others.

I think it was the success of "The Heat is On" that brought Glenn to the attention of the people who were creating the television show *Miami Heat*. They heard "Smuggler's Blues" and decided to write an episode that followed the story in the song, and they asked Glen if he would like a part in the show. In the episode, Crockett and Tubbs (who are Miami Vice) are recruited by the DEA to bust some smugglers who are smuggling drugs into Miami. Glenn plays one of the smugglers who agrees to help the cops. And, of course, we get to hear the song as part of the episode.

Miami Vice liked Glenn's work enough that he wrote another song for the series. "You Belong to the City" was used in the program in 1985 and was the second of Glenn's solo work to reach number two on the charts. It is also part of the *Miami Vice Soundtrack* which includes the "Miami Vice Theme" by Jan Hammer. This single was a number one song and the last instrumental of the rock era to hit number one of which I am aware. The album Soundtrack also hit number one and was the bestselling album of the year 1985.

Glenn was now seen as an actor after appearing on *Miami Vice* and got roles in several different television shows over the next few years. He appeared in the movie *Let's Get Harry* which was released in 1986. He had a bit part in *Jerry Maguire* playing opposite Tom Cruise. He also appeared in the television show *Wiseguys* and actually got the starring role in a show called *South of Sunset* in 1993. *South of Sunset*, unfortunately only aired one episode and was quickly cancelled. Glenn's acting career ended on a negative note.

However, Glenn didn't mind. He was getting tired of acting, anyway, and music was still his first love. In 1988, he released *Soul Searchin'* which was pretty much panned by the critics and didn't sell as well as his previous efforts, peaking at only thirty six on the charts. It produced one single "True Love" which reached number thirteen on the Top 40. "True Love" would be Glenn's last Top 40 single as a solo artist.

In 1986, Glenn got a wake-up call. He came down with diverticulitis which is an ailment where pouches form on the inside of your colon and it is extremely painful. It was bad enough that he had to be hospitalized for a few days. Glenn saw this as a warning and decided to clean up. He stopped taking drugs and started a fitness program. He's still alive today, probably because of the steps he took back then.

This is said to be the motivation behind the song "Livin' Right" which is on the *Soul Searchin'* album.

While filming the video for "Livin' Right," Glenn met a dancer named Cindy Mullican. The two went together for a couple years and were married in 1990. They are still together and have three children: two girls and a boy.

22-The Solo Years of the Others

Let's talk about the two that left the band earlier, first.

Bernie Leadon left the spotlight after leaving the Eagles and he went home and laid low for a while. In 1977, he got together with friend Michael Georgiades and they recorded *Natural Progressions* which, to me, sounds a lot like early Eagles. It's a good album, although it wasn't commercially successful, it is still available on Amazon, but you'll pay a hefty price for a new copy.

Bernie continued to perform off and on, but without the success he had with Eagles. He played mostly as a session player and concentrated primarily on country and country-rock. He played with the Nitty Gritty Dirt Band, and he worked with Restless Heart, both country bands. He created a group called Run C&W, a takeoff on the name Run DMC which took R&B songs and refitted them to a country sound. You can find several Run C&W songs on YouTube. Check it out, you'll like it. Bernie is still active today, although not as much as he used to be.

Randy Meisner created his own band after leaving the Eagles and, in 1978, he released his first solo album, *Randy Meisner*. The album barely made it into the Hot 100, peaking at 94. It's interesting to me that he included "Take It to the Limit," the song he sang lead on for Eagles on his first solo album. The song is the same, yet different. The magic of the Eagles is, somehow, missing. His second album in 1980 was *One More Song* which did a little better than the first, peaking at number fifty. He spent most of the Eighties as a session musician with other bands. He worked with James Taylor, Joe Walsh, Dan Fogelberg, and many others.

I can't leave Randy without telling the story of his impostor. This is one of those crazy things that happen to famous people. A man named

Lewis Peter "Buddy" Morgan decided one day to pretend he was Randy Meisner. He had done the same thing as Don Henley in Las Vegas but had jumped bail when they tried to arrest him. Anyway, this Morgan guy travels around saying he is Randy Meisner. My understanding is that he kind of looked like him and had false documents printed up that claimed he really was Randy. He successfully got away with his charade until 1977 when they arrested him and he spent 16 months in jail for his crimes.

What did he do when he got out of jail? He went right back to being Randy again and was still doing it in 2009, although by that time most hotels had caught on to the act, and he wasn't as successful. It takes all kinds.

Don Felder went home and spent time with his family after leaving the group. As I've mentioned before, Don was a great guitar player but was not recognized as a singer, so it was hard to put out a solo album of just guitar work. He worked with the Bee Gees, Diana Ross, and Barbra Streisand, and he played for Stevie Nicks on several of her albums.

He spent much of the Eighties working on movie Soundtracks. His playing can be heard in *Heavy Metal* (1981) as well as Neil Simon's *The Slugger's Wife* (1985) and a 1985 romantic comedy *Secret Admirer*. From 1985 to 1986, he played in his own television show FTV which was a sketch comedy series that essentially made fun of MTV videos. I don't remember the show at all, so it either played in another country or didn't make an impact here in the United States, because I watched a lot of TV in the Eighties.

Don did, in fact, release a solo album in 1983 called *Airborne*. I listened to a few songs from this album, and I'm convinced Don got a raw deal from the guys in Eagles. I think his voice is as good as most rock performers I've heard. *Airborne* is a solid effort and should have done much better than it did. Vendors on Amazon want $208 for a new copy of the CD, so I guess I won't be listening to the whole thing any time soon.

It wasn't until 2012, nearly thirty years later, that Don released a second solo album, *Road to Forever*. This album received a lot of praise when it came out, and I've listened to a couple of cuts from it. This is a great album, and the good part is, it's only $9.99 on Amazon. I'm getting out my credit card. This is too good to pass up. I hope the world admits that Don Felder is a master. His work is top notch and while he didn't get along with Glenn Frey sometimes, he was part of one of the greatest bands in American history and has proven himself as a solo artist as well.

Joe Walsh had done solo work before he joined the Eagles and so it was easy to go back to that after the breakup. As a joke, Joe announced he was running for President in 1980. He wasn't old enough to actually take the job if he had won (which was unlikely), but he had fun campaigning. He promised to make "Life's Been Good" the country's national anthem and he promised free gas for everyone if he was elected. Like the others, he continued to record albums into the Eighties but didn't have a lot of commercial success. He spent a couple of years in Australia, from 1984-1985. He performed with an Australian band called Party Boys.

In 1989, after coming back from Australia, he toured with Ringo Starr for a while and then did an *MTV Unplugged* with the legendary Dr. John. I recently saw him do a special with Paul McCartney, and he played with Kenny Chesney on CMT's *Crossroads* show.

Next, Joe got together with some real legends in the rock business. The group was called The Best, and it truly was. He played with Keith Emerson who was a founder of Emerson, Lake, and Palmer, a great band from the early Seventies; John Entwistle who was a part of The Who, and you don't get any bigger than that; Jeff "Skunk" Baxter who played with Steely Dan and the Doobie Brothers; and lastly Simon

Phillips, a drummer who also played with The Who and various other groups.

Timothy B Schmit like the others began a solo career after the breakup. Mostly, he worked with other groups as a session player. He has a very nice voice and can be heard as a background singer in several songs during the Eighties. He sang on Bob Seger's "Fire Lake" and Boz Scaggs' "Look What You've Done to Me" (Don Henley and Glenn Frey also sang on that record, so it was almost an Eagles reunion). He sang harmony on Crosby, Stills, and Nash's "Southern Cross." He also worked with Don Felder on "Heavy Metal."

Now, I assume that the music community in California was not that big in the Eighties, and it was inevitable that the guys would run into each other, but I think it's great that they were good enough friends or professional enough that they could get together during these projects without tearing each other's faces off. Evidence of this, I've already described, but he also played and sang on Don Henley's "Dirty Laundry" and "You Don't Know Me At all," the latter was included on Henley's Greatest Hits album.

As further proof of this, he got together with Randy Meisner and Joe Walsh to backup Richard Marx on his song "Don't Mean Nothing." He worked with Toto on several of their hits in the mid-Eighties. From 1983-1985, he toured with Jimmy Buffet and was a member of the Coral Reef Band (Buffet's band.) Timothy is responsible for coining the term "Parrotheads" which refers to Buffet's fans.

Timothy released five solo albums after the split with the band. None of them charted very well, and three of them didn't chart at all. *Playin' It Cool* (1984) and *Timothy B.* (1987) both made the Hot 200 on Billboard but were way down over one hundred. He peaked at number twenty five on the singles charts with "Boys Night Out" from the *Timothy B.* album, but that is his only single to chart.

23-"Hell Freezes Over"

It was said during the Eighties that the Eagles would never get back together. Don Henley had said that the Eagles would get back together when Hell freezes over. Well, in 1994, it happened.

It almost happened in 1990, when four of the five got together and rehearsed for a few days, but when Glenn Frey was asked to be a part of it, he refused. Without the support of Glenn, the whole idea just fell apart. They went their separate ways again.

A lot of the credit for the reunion can be given to Travis Tritt, the country singer. In late 1993, a project was proposed as a tribute to the Eagles. *Common Thread: The Songs of the Eagles* was produced with Eagles songs, each being done by a different country singer. Much of the proceeds of the album would go to the Walden Woods Project, which was the brainchild of Don Henley. The purpose of the Walden Woods project was to purchase and protect the land around the area of Walden Pond where Henry David Thoreau did his writing. Don had heard that developers were set to go in and tear up the woods for some project and he said, "Not if I can help it!"

Travis Tritt was to sing the song "The Long Run," and he said he would do it only if the members of Eagles would join him on the song and in the video. Don Henley, Glenn Frey, Don Felder, Joe Walsh, and Timothy B Schmit agreed to do it (I'm not sure if they asked Randy and Bernie, but they did not take part.) Glenn only agreed to do it this time because it was for a charity he believed in. The five came into the studio together for the first time in thirteen years and helped Tritt record the song. They had so much fun doing it and all five of them realized that old animosities were behind them. It was time for a reunion.

Manager Irving Azoff knew he had to have either Don Felder or Joe Walsh in the reunion band and hopefully, both. They asked Don, and he said yes right away, but Joe Walsh was in bad shape in 1994. He was on drugs and an alcoholic, and no one was sure he could do the job, so someone went to Joe and bodily drove him to a rehab center. Joe made a commitment to clean up and be in the band again. Now he had something he hadn't had in a long time: a reason to get clean and sober, and he did.

The very first time they performed before an audience in fourteen years was at an MTV concert which was taped on April 25 and 26, 1994 in Burbank, California. During a new song they had just wrote, "Learn to Be Still", Don Henley, singing lead, forgot the words to the song. There was this pause when all the instruments are playing, but no vocal and suddenly everyone in the band is laughing and the audience loves it. The ice was broken and the group suddenly felt together as they hadn't in years.

Thus, the "Hell Freezes Over" tour was proposed and from 1994 until 1996 the Eagles were back. The tour spawned a live album by the same name, *Hell Freezes Over*, which debuted at number one on the album charts. It even contained a couple of new studio recordings which were released as singles. "Get Over It" (#31) was the first song written by the Frey/Henley team in many years. "Love Will Keep Us Alive" did not appear on the Hot 100 chart, but it did hit number one on Billboard's Adult Contemporary Charts and was twenty two on the Airplay Chart. I guess the Eagles now appealed more to the adult audience or the people that grew up with them than the general record buying public. Glenn Frey made the comment, "We were now adult rock stars."

In 1998, the event every Eagles fan had waited for happened. The band was inducted into the Rock and Roll Hall of Fame. For the first time ever, all seven of the members of Eagles were together on the same stage. They did two songs, "Take It Easy" and "Hotel California."

The five continued to tour for the next several years. It was good to be back. There was no pressure on the group. They could participate in the touring and still be involved in personal projects and do solo albums if they desired. But all was not well in paradise.

When the reunion was proposed, Glenn said he would not be a part of it unless he and Don Henley received a bigger share than the rest of the guys. After all, their careers had continued to grow after the breakup while the other three had just tread water during those fourteen years. This was OK with everyone except Don Felder. The old feelings he and Glenn had had were starting to resurface and as the tour continued, Felder got more and more unhappy.

There was a lot of complaining. Felder thought he should be paid the same as everyone else, and Glenn told him it just wasn't going to happen. Finally, on February 6, 2001, Don Felder was fired from the group. Now, they were four again. Don Felder said it just broke his heart, and he proceeded to sue the band or actually the legal entity "Eagles Ltd.," for unlawful termination and breach of contract. Eagles Ltd., countersued and the case was in court for several years until, in 2007, they settled out-of-court for an undisclosed amount. Felder wrote a tell-all book in 2007 called *Heaven and Hell: My Life in the Eagles (1974-2001)* which is still available on Amazon.

What a shame that pride can get in the way of a relationship and destroy it. Don Felder has never played with the band since and probably never will. Steuart Smith, who was a well-known guitarist and session player, was hired to take Don Felder's place.

A record that needs to be noted is "Hole in the World". This was the first song recorded without Don Felder. It was released right after 9-11 in response to the attack. The song was released first as a DVD single and then included on the album *The Very Best of* in 2003. It is also included as a bonus track on their next album, *Long Road Out of Eden*.

24-"Long Road Out of Eden"

In 2007, the guys decided if they were going to be a real band, they couldn't depend on their oldies to keep them going. They wrote their first album of all new material since 1979. The album *Long Road Out of Eden* was the first album from a major group to be distributed by a retail outlet. Initially, it was only sold in Wal-Mart and did not have a distributor. The album debuted at number one in late 2007.

Some of the highlights of this album are "How Long" which is a song written by their old friend J.D. Souther back in the Seventies, but the Eagles had never covered it so now they did. "Busy Being Fabulous" is another cool song from the album that was written by Don Henley. It did not chart on the pop charts but did reach number twenty eight on the Billboard Country Songs chart.

Another song which I really like is "No More Walks in the Wood" in which Don Henley put music to a poem by American poet John Hollander. The song relates to Don's work with the Walden Woods Project.

From March 20, 2008 when they launched their "Long Road Out of Eden" tour in London until May 9, 2009 when they wrapped it up in Sandy, Utah, which is right down the road from me, they toured and promoted the album. All of the remaining four members are now in their sixties, and it's not evident just how long they can do this. That tour was supposed to be the last but in 2013, they announced another "final" tour of the Eagles. They are on the road right now (as I write this in the summer of 2013) and just a couple weeks ago they added ten or twelve new shows to the list of venues where they would play.

25-LEGACY OF THE EAGLES

They claim that their 1976 album *Eagles – Their Greatest Hits 1971-1975* is the best-selling album of the Twentieth Century. On November 10, 1999, it surpassed Michael Jackson's *Thriller* as the best-selling album of the century. Since then, due to the death of Michael Jackson, I think the album has slipped to second place for bestselling of all time.

They are ranked as number 23 of VH1's Greatest Artists of Rock & Roll. *Hotel California*, the album, is ranked by VH1 as #38 of the 100 Greatest Albums, and VH1 ranks the song "Hotel California" as #6 of the Greatest Rock Songs.

The Eagles are the third bestselling group in American history, and it's interesting to note that number one and two, The Beatles and Led Zeppelin, are both British groups.

As mentioned before, the entire group, all seven, were inducted into the Rock & Roll Hall of Fame in 1998.

The phrase "Life in the Fast Lane" was introduced into popular culture by an Eagles song.

The Eagles band has won six Grammy Awards. In 1975, "Lyin' Eyes" won *Best Pop Vocal Performance by a Duo, Group, or Chorus*. In 1977, the single "Hotel California" won for record of the year, and "New Kid in Town" won *Best Arrangement for Voices*. In 1979, "Heartache Tonight" won *Best Rock Vocal Performance by a Duo, Group, or Chorus*. In 2008, "How Long" won *Best Country Performance By A Duo Or Group With Vocals*. And, last but not least, in 2009, "I Dreamed There Was No War" won *Best Pop Instrumental Performance*.

26-AFTERWORD

The Eagles band is certainly one of the great American bands. They have been together, more or less, for over forty years. Not many bands can say that. I was fortunate enough to see them in 2005 when they played Salt Lake City. I missed them when they came back in 2009, and I regret that now.

I just read that The Eagles will be playing this coming October (2013) in Dallas, Texas on their most recent final reunion tour. My daughter lives in Texas. Maybe it's time for me to go visit her.

Are the members of Eagles really done? No one knows. I would watch them forever and hope they continue to tour and make new records, but, of course, that is up to them. Good luck guys. Keep making us all happy.

Don Henley once said, "At the end of the day, it was and still is about the music." Amen to that.

You can contact me at www.number1project.com where I occasionally blog about things that interest me in the music world (mostly, the twentieth century). Go find it and read it and leave me a comment. I also have a Facebook fan page called "Legends of Rock & Roll". "Like" me and comment there, too. If you love the music as much as I do, you'll enjoy the trip. Thanks for reading.

I hope you have enjoyed this book as much as I have enjoyed writing it for you.

If you have liked what you read, will you please do me a favor and leave a review of "Eagles". Thank you.

About the Author

James Hoag has always been a big fan of Rock & Roll. Most people graduate from high school and then proceed to "grow up" and go on to more adult types of music. James got stuck at about age 18 and has been an avid fan of popular music ever since. His favorite music is from the Fifties, the origin of Rock & Roll and which was the era in which James grew up. But he likes almost all types of popular music including country music.

After working his entire life as a computer programmer, he is now retired and he decided to share his love of the music and of the performers by writing books that discuss the life and music of the various people who have meant so much to him over the years.

He calls each book a "love letter" to the stars that have enriched our lives so much. These people are truly Legends.

SELECTED DISCOGRAPHY

Studio Albums

1972 – Eagles
1973 – Desperado
1974 – On the Border
1975 – One of These Nights
1976 – Hotel California
1979 – The Long Run
2007 – Long Road Out of Eden

Live Albums

1980 – Eagles Live
1994 – Hell Freezes Over
2005 – Farewell 1 Tour-Live from Melbourne

Singles

1972 – "Take It Easy"
1972 – "Witchy Woman"
1972 – "Peaceful Easy Feeling"
1973 – "Tequila Sunrise"
1973 – "Outlaw Man"
1974 – "Already Gone"
1974 – "James Dean"
1974 – "Best of My Love"
1975 – "One of These Nights"
1975 – "Lyin' Eyes"
1975 – "Take It to the Limit"
1976 – "New Kid in Town"
1977 – "Hotel California"
1977 – "Life in the Fast Lane"

1978 – “Please Come Home for Christmas”
1979 – “Heartache Tonight”
1979 – “The Long Run”
1980 – “I Can't Tell You Why”
1980 – “Seven Bridges Road”
1994 – “Get Over It”
1994 – “Love Will Keep Us Alive”
1994 – “The Girl from Yesterday”
1995 – “Learn to Be Still”
2003 – “Hole in the World”
2005 – “No More Cloudy Days”
2007 – “How Long”
2008 – “Busy Being Fabulous”
2008 – “What Do I Do with My Heart”
2009 – “I Don't Want to Hear Any More”

15586141R00040

Printed in Great Britain
by Amazon